The
COOKE BOOK:
A Seasoning of Poets

The
COOKE BOOK:
A Seasoning of Poets

Edited by Michael S. Glaser

SCOP Eleven
SCOP Publications, Inc.
College Park, Maryland

Made possible in part by a grant from Maryland State Arts Council, and financial help from St. Mary's College, St. Mary's, Maryland and the St. Mary's Arts Council. Appreciation is extended to Friends of SCOP for donations: Shirley Cochrane, Carolyn Kreiter-Kurylo, Elaine Magarrell, Betty Parry, Kathy Pearce-Lewis, Anne R. Prange, Robert Sargent, Helen Wesley, and others who wish to remain anonymous.

Cover art by Judith Hall

Library of Congress Cataloging-in-Publication Data

The Cooke book.

Collection of poems that have been read during the
past ten years at the Ebenezer Cooke Poetry Festival,
St. Mary's College of Maryland.
1. American poetry—Washington Metropolitan Area.
2. American poetry—20th century.   I. Glaser, Michael S.,
1943-   II. Ebeneezer Cooke Poetry Festival.
PS548. D6C6   1987   81'.54'0809753   87-14143
ISBN 0-930526-10-4

SCOP ELEVEN in a series
Printed in the United States of America
SCOP Publications, Inc.
Box #376, College Park, Maryland 20740

INTRODUCTION

The Ebenezer Cooke Poetry Festival began in 1976 as a part of the emerging St. Mary's Summer Festival, sponsored by the St. Mary's Creative Arts Forum and funded by grants from the Maryland Arts Council and the St. Mary's County Commissioners. Named after the first poet laureate of Maryland, Ebenezer Cooke, the Festival was begun, in part, to commemorate the spirit of the man who, when commissioned by Charles Calvert, third Lord Baltimore, to write a poem praising the Mary-Land colony as a place "beauteous beyond description . . . majestic in her past and glorious in her future," wrote instead "The Sotweed Factor"—an overly long narrative poem telling how foul he found life in Mary-Land, a place of "Regions waste/ Where No Man's Faithful, Nor a Woman Chaste."

The connection between the past and the present as they are linked by the arts brought the St. Mary's City Commission, the St. Mary's Arts Forum and St. Mary's College of Maryland together with the idea of inviting poets from around the state of Maryland to come to the site of the first settlement in Maryland (as well as her first capital) to celebrate both poets and poetry and also to share with the guest poets the inspirational environment of St. Mary's City.

For its first two years, the Cooke Festival was run as an open reading, after which the gathered poets would adjourn to a local bar to continue the readings and festivities into the night. One of the more memorable highlights of those early years was the time a lonely, drunken sailor from the nearby Naval Air Station wandered into the reading and asked what was going on. When he learned it was a poetry reading, he stood up in front of the audience and recited from memory more verses than anyone cared to hear about a lost love in his life. While his poem reminded many of us of Ebenezer Cooke's overly long complaint about life in the new colony, we also delighted in the fact that this sailor was moved by the opportunity to share his feelings and experiences with a community of others who valued poetry.

As the Ebenezer Cooke Poetry Festival evolved, we began to have to limit the number of poets as well as the length of the readings—though we still hold on to Josiah Royce's notion that when you don't find your beloved community you must create it—and we see the Cooke Festival as one small way of fostering and supporting that community of poets who seek—in any number and variety of voices and forms—to give shape and expression to their experiences through poetry.

The Ebenezer Cooke Poetry Festival traditionally took place in the reconstructed Statehouse in St. Mary's City, though one year it was held in the Trinity Church on the original site of Maryland's first statehouse. In 1984, for the first time, the Festival took place in the newly constructed "17th century Inn" in St. Mary's City, where air-conditioning, despite its anomalous nature, provided a welcomed addition that has been continued as the Festival moved into the newly constructed Fine Arts Building, Montgomery Hall, of St. Mary's College. Since 1980, a crab feast has followed the festival—the poets and their guests gathering to eat, meet, renew friendships and discuss poetry on the banks of the St. Mary's River where Maryland's first settlers landed over 350 years ago.

Funds to support the Ebenezer Cooke Poetry Festival have come from the Maryland State Arts Council, the St. Mary's Arts Council, the St. Mary's City Commission, St. Mary's College of Maryland and the proceeds of the Chaucer Award which is sponsored by the Festival of Poets and Poetry at St. Mary's College—though without the help of "in-kind" services from the St. Mary's City Commission and St. Mary's College of Maryland in providing hours and hours of staff support, space for the reading, help with catering and housing, equipment, xeroxing, phone calls, mail, etc. etc., the Cooke Festival would simply not be possible. There is even a wonderful old waterman in St. Mary's County, Mr. Lloyd Bowles, who has helped by catching and steaming the crabs we eat at the crab feast following the reading.

One person deserves special mention: Charlie Hewitt, the founder and former director of the St. Mary's Creative Arts Forum, whose idea the Cooke Festival originally was, and who provided the energy, direction and impetus to get the Ebenezer Cooke Poetry Festival off the ground. Charlie is forever the kind of spirit who seeks to build community, and whose "why not—Let's do it!" has done more than most anyone realizes to make St. Mary's City an exciting cultural center during the hot and lazy Maryland summers. The Ebenezer Cooke Poetry Festival is one small corner of his legacy, and the growing community of poets and lovers of poetry who look forward each year to the Cooke Festival, participate in his vision of building community in much the same way as the early settlers who first came to Maryland en-visioned a new community of tolerance and freedom.

* * * * *

This anthology represents the variety of poetic voices, forms, styles and subjects of the wide cross-section of poets who have participated in the Ebenezer Cooke Poetry Festival since its beginning. Every effort was made to solicit poems from each of the poets who have participated in the Cooke Festival since 1976, and most all of the poets who have read are included in this volume.

Special appreciation is due to SCOP Publications, Inc. and its editorial board for their enthusiasm and commitment to this anthology. Stacy Tuthill, Founder and President of SCOP, and Charles Rossiter have put in many long hours seeing this book through to completion. Judith Hall provided inval-uable editorial assistance and Mark D'Datto, Lisa Miller, Maja Prausnitz and

Jenne Whited have all contributed significantly to the many tasks that are involved in putting together a work of this sort.

Finally, I want to express appreciation to the Maryland State Arts Council, the St. Mary's Arts Council and St. Mary's College of Maryland for the grants which have enabled us to publish this book.

Michael S. Glaser
St. Mary's City
1987

CONTENTS

MY FATHER (in a chair)

for my brother
(who never understood)

I shaped his face
and he held the pose
like the photo of his monkey
shoulder-sitting
juxtaposed with
his large beard
now diminished
to a mustache
South America
a faraway light
in his green eyes
I will go
slicing off
a chunk of time
like chocolate
he can slide
between his teeth
the word, "Brazil"
he says it like
no one else does

"GOE FROM MY WINDOW"

an Elizabethan lute song

The light of this memory's sky
is always blue
as I lean against the cedar
and you in a time unbound
sit with your quiet guitar to bring forth
the quick sounds of love and love denying.
Go from my window.
She is hollow, shaped to sing.
Hold her. Your moving hands, her emptiness
will make the song.
Here beneath the timeless dome
you stay and go, you never leave.
We are young, and always will be
in the summer light, in the fragrant wood.
Turned away from me, angular but graceful
with the gentleness, the urgency of this pursuit,
you find the song in the air between us,
set it trembling, tell me, never tell me
if this is love.

UNTITLED

I heard an owl call as I left the house
In this morning's early darkness.
A man once told me, saying he knew about owls,
That they only call in the late Spring.
It's a mating call, he said.

But this is December, even if unseasonably warm,
And there was—if it is indeed a mating call—no answer.

The other theory is that the call
Is to startle some night forager,
A mouse, perhaps, or raccoon.

I don't know the truth;
Except I did hear an owl call this morning,
Alone in the warm, foggy December air,
Both out of season and out of place,
Adrift, like me, in the long dark nights.

TANKERS

for Tara Siobhan Beall

These lights, as cities' harborings
of distant coasts, trace silently the horizon's
and their own communion. No less an intricate pattern
than the lacewing's goes beyond the grove of tall pines.
Incessantly as the pounding of surf, again and again
without comment they pass to destinations burdened
by the curve of earth.

Triangulations of the shifting land
and the stars' arcs guide them. Echoes
that probe beneath their oceans tell of the contours
there. What lost Atlantis flecks from time to time
their deeps may make stories for children told at the bell
of a closing day. For now, the mariners' faces
are lit with the instruments' dim, red glow.

Of the imperatives that launch them
and set their course beyond, into the reach
of their own mythologies, there is no clue.
These gossamer networks, half metallic, half light,
winking in and out beyond the trees, and our conjectures
here, based on imperfect knowledge, lead us to beliefs
certain as beacons on a rocky shore, where waves'
tumults finger the white air into a kind of song.

IRELAND

Scratch out the line
as soon as write it—
        all the wrongs that long
        a rightness:
Celt cross, shattered
whiskey bottle shoved in chest,
        these green quavering hills, all
        portioned in my blood, bullets
ward & precinct
taking no love at love
        sobbing for a song
        about mother & home
at war with
my very charming self

FORCES OF NATURE I

Questions like: do angels have wings, these are the kind of things
we demand answers to—and do they really fly into our dreams
with their array of doors, towers, baskets, rivers, radiators
and snakes just to show how we've been bad again;
don't they have anything good to say;
why do they appear in pillars of smoke, pillars of light;
are they afraid to show their faces, or is the task
merely to keep us guessing—do they bite?
and how many of these infernal creatures are dancing
to beat the band on the stainless steel dance floor,
manic as usual at God's bidding, and why doesn't he do his own
dirty work, anyway, why doesn't he fight his own battles
and not draft us and his poor angels to blow until we're blue,
why do we continue to hope we were made in his own image
when all we know for sure is
we can dance like angels and we don't stop
whispering, "fools, what fools," as we float away.

LINEAGE

Oh, the parade, the father climbing after himself
the eldest calling wait, wait, see me, see me
the middle child tumbling out of her moment of sun
the youngest he'll never catch up never catch up
out of the basement of the clapboard house
out of the roots and twigs of the once-bright nest
where she still guards the eggs, puts worms in their mouths
and says this is what matters the nest the nest
I'll give you the nest I never had I'll bring back my dead mother
she'll mother us all she'll mother us all
come back stop climbing come back stop climbing come back

He died in Chicago I knew he'd do it to me
out of his basement he climbed after himself
just as his father before him his mother gripping her twigs
this is what matters she said the nest the nest
climb but not far climb but not far
up the ladder of business of lodges of leaders
because this is what matters the nest the nest
you can climb just don't fly you can climb just don't fly
this is what matters the nest the nest

He climbed after himself
oh, the parade, the father heading toward his light
the eldest calling wait, wait, I'm right behind
see me see me
the middle child tumbling out of her moment of sun
the youngest he'll never catch up never catch up
because this is what matters the nest the nest

WITH SURE CONFIDENCE

for ABS

Day springs gray and wet.
In growing light, I sit
on the dock. Soft winter
rain whispers away my tears.

Why should I weep?
Why should I sit on the dock in the rain?

The tide is low. The creek is
silver-green. On the far side,
a woman calls her dog. Wild
ducks swim at the bend. Near
the bank, a blue heron stalks
the reeds. The tide changes.

For joy in the morning.
For love of the tide.

Silently, how silently,
the day breaks, the tide rises.

The joy that I can voice
is not the joy.
The love that I can say
is not the love.

THE CLAM BAR

I

here
you can find
people on the half-shell:
        steamin,
        or bubblin,
        or floatin in soup.

        people with pinball eyes
        who listen to tom waits,
        play loud, jivin pitch,
        and inhale their unemployment checks thru
        beer mugs they clutch for warmth
        from winter
        at the icehands of lake ontario.

II

patrons of the clam bar
write graffitti on the ladies' room walls.
i study it like i once studied algebra:
        both teach you to think
        in a certain pattern.

"MY MOTHER MADE ME A LESBIAN. . . ."
    i can't decipher the rest;
      the equation i can't solve—
        the one i want so much
          to figure out.

"LSD consumes 47 times its weight
in excess reality."

excess reality
there's a lotta that goin around.
the clam bar
with its clientele,
its music,
its live-in connections,
shrinks oversized reality
to manageable proportions.

HARRIET TUBMAN SAID

There are many kinds of being scared:
hiding out with snakes in a swamp,
praying in a whisper so low the Lord
strains to hear; and in morning light
all gold and flashy, you trample down
marshweed beside the road, shivering at
every bird call; or you hold on
to some long, way-back love, wishing
against all odds your name will come up
on his lips; sometimes it's a brief glimpse
of old square-toed death, reared-up
on his hind legs, waiting.

My train only moves one way and it's up
a mountain. You left fear standing
in a field with a whip; he was your
running start. Now he's sniffing around,
licking your heels, tasting your sweat.
You turn and I see him behind your eyes;
he suits you fine 'cause he's all you had
for so long. But I'll tell you this,
you can't go back. Fear will never be
so close to you as this cold, iron finger
I hold in your ear. You can only die once.
You can die now, or you can be free.

**FROM:
ANIMAS EN PENA
(SOULS IN PAIN)**

#3

an indian is playing a flute
in the mountains in Chihuahua
a lament of monotony

> indios speak
> only your own language
> indios sleep
> only with your own women
> indios remember
> your dead have
> not a home

a hot wind bows the pinion pine
in the mountains in Chihuahua
the nuts rattle
in the cones
        and fall

THREE WOMEN SWIMMING A RIVER

Only the *ghosts* of jelly fish remain
forming like semen for next year's assault.
A large school of spot make a V
just under the water, turning sideways
to flash their silver knives. "Schooling
fish are not biting fish," one of our husbands
once said.

And which of us, we ask ourselves
as we walk into water, putting
feet carefully onto what feels
like a long-submerged water buffalo—
which of us ever got enough
of any man's wisdom before he
took off to be buried, or married
to someone else?

Which man ever proved he would not
be bled to death by mosquitoes?
Or told us why there are ribbons
of dark and light, cold and sun
in this water?

They left before we learned
that the fine sand ringing
the far bank is really broken
shells and bottles like ones
we cut our feet on at home
dock or that water, pure blue
at the horizon line, is brown
as water we've left behind, now
transformed from this distance
into flawless blue.

CHILD IN A STRAW HAT

(Painting by Mary Cassatt, circa 1886)

Clockface open at breakfast
Father refolds the morning
talk clinking muffining around
until he bolts
to the real commerce
of tapes ticking yes-no
to his Railroad

Tricked again   again
tricked she was to ride stand sit
as one who owns and knows
and like him
is   But she
a watchcase not knowing
the golden chain she graces

Engraved beneath
her mother's yellow straw hat
small face folding
to shoulders rounding to hands
betrayed   she gazes
still gazes
after the receding moment

ODE TO A DOG

To Daddy's Little Girl—Czarina

How well remembers
my heart
toddling about
under the spacious
rambling rose
of Millstone Landing
headquarters being
the dog house.
Then up through
the swiftening years.
Along with me
so frequently
a dog.
Many the kind,
much varied the size,
color, frame.
We have sat
at each other's feet.
Such companionship.
Even some heart breaking miles
have been made
more gentle, even sweet.
There's a time to coast.
There's a time to bark.
There's a time to bite.
There's a time
to chase buzzards,
and a time
to sit on the porch.

Then also "Aw Shucks".
If we will listen
we, too, can learn.

I, a simple common man
speak
for many men
and boys,
and women
and girls,
and even presidents
as
I thank The Great All Father
for moments
made terrific
and years made memorable
by the presence
of a dog.
(even with fleas).

As I step
into the sunset years
I pray
that henceforth
with me
to the end,
O God,
may there be
a dog,
to be loved by
another
when I bow out.

AMONG OTHER PLACES THEY LEAVE THEIR BODIES

on the lawn; a child's air glider
still gliding with weight of the child;
at this house, and at the beach house
on dock pilings, on the far shore.

Among other places they rise up through floor boards
breaks in foundations.

First, a carapace fused over the pupa; now it's an
old woman whose hands bother her
what are they giving away   what are they holding—

embrace that goes on and on
as if patient, as if they couldn't help it this
grappling with absence, brown shell
brittle as a hip.

Eyes like that, what are they trained on
only what's distant, what moves?
I've heard the dead used to outnumber us only now
we've pulled ahead, we're winning   why—
when the child comes in to surprise us
cupping the locust shell—

this tension along the spine this tearing
this impulse to grip.

—ORPHEUS SEPARATES
THE BACON FROM THE EGGS—

As the world is divided into
      left and right
      I clap my hands
      and expect the band
      to march in, the music
      to begin

As the poles are pointed
      north and south
      with neither east nor west
      for compromise
      I wait for the geese
      to fly, seeking mothers,
      native lakes, the north star

As the cycle is divided into
      day and night
      I set the alarm clock
      for 'must'—and pull
      the shades

As self divides into
      'this' and 'that'
      I meet Narcissus in the
      mirror as I shave
      and Eurydice leaps onto
      the subway behind me.

DAVE

we slipped naked,
silent as lone wolves,
cresting a stream,
the words
stuck in the throat.
we were loons,
following an Eternal
arc—sun tattled time
like children at
Christmas,
counted minutes like
sand, trapped
motionless inside the hour-
glass.

Herons flocked the
shore,
beaks pushed deep
into Potomac
mud; there was even
a mystery—was that
a muskrat,
riding the Towpath?
feet scraped clean
by nettles hiding
in the tall
grass. or something hidden
deeper?
an eel
locked in prehistoric

ice? a dragon, oozing
fire, wily
sea-drake
spitting poison?
as we drifted,
drank up all
the wine,
then jettisoned
like crazy fliers
back down-
stream—making
history in the desert
in the '50's—we
dipped a dusty
wing.

STILL

Today's paper carries this headline:
"Fading Taste For Bourbon Pinches Kentucky."
But a distiller named Bill Samuels, Jr.
Is not concerned, saying the market
Has always had its highs and lows, and besides,
He says, though his is a small company
With sales of only 125,000 cases a year,
He's doing fine: "We sell out of whiskey
Every year, and you can hardly beat that
When everybody's wringing their hands."

His own brand is Maker's Mark,
His "Family has made whiskey for four
Generations near Bardstown," Kentucky
And he tells the family story:
How an ancestor was mustered out of
The Revolutionary War in 1793,
Moved to Kentucky, and turned to whiskey.
Land was offered to anyone who would settle,
Raise corn, and stay 3 years. "This,"
Says Samuels, "was most attractive to people
Who knew what to do with corn . . .
They started making whiskey
And that was the first money of the west."

This story in the Lynchburg *News*
Soaks in a high-mash flavor, which just
Hints that if our taste is fading
It's because our tongues and palates
Have been bleached by pacific chablis,
Dulled by low-cal reds
And washed out by bad lite beer.

While "pinches Kentucky" gauges a slack
In the belly of the country's swagger,
As still hands are laid off
And recession more than taste trickles dry
down the mean alembics of the time.
Next the expert American of Mr. Samuels,
Whose border drawl is 200 years
Into the hickory-trough grain of his saying
"We sell out of whiskey," and whose
Work has had no trouble paying off
His father's his and his son's bills.
And so he understands the problem
To be one of quality-control,
Or, as we used to say, know-how:
If all these poor hand-wringing
Sons of whiskey-makers only
Knew what to do with that corn . . . ,
And oak-aged 100-proof canticle
Of knowing what to do with the hands.

And what about *Bards*town?
Was this whiskey town named for a poet?
Or all poets?—I doubt it—
Probably for some John or Henry or Bill Bard.
But this American Samuels and Samuels' son
Has made his name with Maker's Mark, a bourbon
Bearing the poet's verb (poiein) to make:
As if from the secret empty spaces
In that seed kernel of corn
Planted in a dark and bloody ground
By revolutionary regulars, we make
Not only the feed to tame wild turkeys
And the first hard coin of

Our brusquely scalawagging west,
But refine as well, from the corn's raw dream,
A forked white-lightning, home-brewed
Or the straight and sour-mash lyric of our genius
That everclear or red jagging water
River branch and grain
We drink our history in.

THE ENCHANTED FOREST

"I have created
a little path
through my room,"
    she tells me . . .

    She has created a path
    through a forest of
    solitary celebrations.
    I see her with the sun
    filtering through
    masses of philodendron
    and wine bottle boles,
    walking the path
    lightly as a child.

    The dark woods
    will retreat before such—
    the mohair underbrush,
    the spindly chippendales
    on one side—
    the breakfront hollow
    with its 62 owls
    on the other;
    the tea cart will
    assume an open air.

    Her parents will smile
    from old photographs,
    pleased to have found
    one lost all night
    in another dark.

On overcast days
she will sink
to the Audubon floor
and pull about her
all the yellow leaves
of autumn.

We laugh
two solitary children
—meeting suddenly
on a path.

GIRL IN THE MIRROR

There is no effort in the arms
and hands raised to plant the hair
with pins on the head. The neck

pivots pink inside the choker
of pearls. The eyes are hummingbirds
taking the mirror by surprise. The lips

press back ascending waves
of silence. I snap her in
the middle, stuff her gently,

waist down, into a crystal bud
vase, knowing that I will wither
here, severed from any real life.

ARM

Yesterday I studied the contour
of a man's arm at a stoplight.
The light was long, the arm deep brown
and curved like an old banister.

When the light turned, the arm sped out of sight.
The down hair, lightly laced in the wind
disappeared, the glow of sunlight
clinging to skin.

I tried to remember the curve of your arm
or thigh or breast, but could only see
that sculptured shape at the stoplight.
I looked at my own arm, wondering why I never noticed it.

Driving home, I let my arm rest on the edge
of the window. I had never so enjoyed the ride.
Later, when the dishes were washed, you went away

and I studied the hair on my arm in the lamplight
as though it were the skin of a poem.
At breakfast you smiled as I poured coffee,

buttered your toast. When I got in the car, staring
at the unopened window, you said everything
would be fine, but, strapped in by the seatbelt,

I was already thinking of the man in that car,
knowing I would race home that evening
through rush hour traffic to you.

A QUESTION OF AESTHETICS

He never wrote a letter without
the words "despair" or "terror"
as in, "Even as a child I knew
despair," or, "How to turn
this terror into art." How romantic
it seemed then, like living
a Russian novel. His final note
read, "Tell her our relationship
was fully satisfying in every way."

No one ever says how thrilling
pain is, how it takes you like
a lover, how your body cringes
before surrender. At first
you cry no, no, then swoon
into its burly arms. You should see
your open mouth, your breath coming
in harsh gasps. Trust pain to find
the choicest part, the marrow,
and suck out resolve, leaving you
limp. But oh, how you'll sleep.

The only burden heavier than pain
is boredom, want of danger. When I
teach *Anna Karenina* to young girls,
I say, "Every woman should experience
one disastrous love affair and survive."
How like a woman Anna was, to hesitate
because she could not bear to throw

her red purse away. How like a man
he was to put a bullet someplace deadly.
As a woman who's survived, I see boredom
now as comfort, devotion as something
precious, and death in any form,
a slap across the face.

TABOO

I take into silence my silence—what
I will not say,
Watching white leaves in sunlight wave.
I tell myself,
I do not know what to say. What if
All the verbs
Lead only back to me? Would no one be there?
Birds penetrate.
They dart along the old imprinting.
Green odors
Wake and turn. If I approach those wishes,
They talk back
From hiding places—worms emerging
After rain—
And so I sleep, afraid, small again, as I
Would be outside.
Sleep protects the way a window tells you
What to see:
The leaves, more yellow in the moving light.
Sleep tucks sound
Away. "Don't frown when you think,"
My mother said.
She came in with laundry. "Don't frown.
You'll wrinkle your skin."
Sleep helps in simple erasures, though what if
I remember
When the rain stopped and children played along
The rhododendron,
Honeysuckle. I was a girl
In Oklahoma,
Where honeysuckle reached the windows,

And when my father
Watered vines, honey rinsed
The air again.
Perhaps it was then that I became silent
With my father.
I was six and watched from the porch as he
Let the water
Fall over petals and into the little straws
I always slipped
Out, touching honey on my tongue. He smiled
At me, but words—
What word first? And even now, when my father
Holds me, though he
Ages into white and blue, even now, well—
He whispers over
The tablecloth as Mother stacks
Dishes in the kitchen.
"You are like me," he says. "You dream."
Then Mother enters,
Balancing plates and forks, the left-over cake, what
The neighbors say.
"Did you notice the new fence? The birds did."
My father nods.
He looks at me. Through the window, birds call out,
In danger or mating.
If I knew what I heard, I would know what to say.

AT THE SAUNA

We men sit on hot planks
at the sauna and talk
of how hard it is here
in Andalucia to find work.
Where am I from they ask
and when I tell them
they rub their sweaty
fingers together to show
how rich they think I am.
I am not a rich man
and the sweat runs down
into my eyes until I weep
and the men shift positions
as someone tosses more
water on the hot rocks
and the sweat pours down
all our bodies. There is
not enough work in Andalucia
and the water in the shower
is always cold. As I sit
shivering on the cold boards
in the drying room and watch
the steam rise from my body
I think of a woman who will
never come to Andalucia
and as the men keep on talking
I know for certain that I
am not a rich man.

CAPTAIN SPEAKING

People dream of flying.
I dreamed I heard
"This is your captain speaking"
in the voice of Ann Darr.
I breathed easy,
knowing I was in good hands.

I was flying in training class,
learning how to enjoy flying
again
after not flying for a long time.

The voice told me to relax,
to enjoy the view,
and to trust my pilot
and the laws of aerodynamics.

I have loved that voice
since a time before I first heard it.
I followed instructions
and came in for landing with a poem.

COMING TO POWER

for Mary Edsall

Each motion of the dark sea
Wants to be a sound she makes,
Wants, and tries to shape itself
In consonants and vowels,
To give her a different taste of time
And of time's other shape, space—
But she, wrapped in her need for details,
Doesn't listen. The sea says
There are forces she cannot imagine,
Forces to be given voice through her body,
Like the voices of sailors drowned at sea
Still heard ashore—in dreams—
Or the cries of a woman absorbed by a wall
When her newborn lies cold, growing colder.
She will not listen. She waits like a widow
For her life to take up its knitting,
For clouds and rain or the cessation of rain
To present change. She would like to move
Fluidly, speaking with her hips and belly,
The bell curve and heave of her breasts,
But the sea and the sea's echo
Do not chime through her deliberate speech,
Nor through the slow plow of her thighs
Along a sea of summer streets.

THE SEPARATION

At this cooling distance of time,
I come back again to the year
of our dislocation. I was fifteen,
not really a man, but old enough
to weather out the long heart-gale
of their shouting, to lean like a young
well rooted tree for the time ahead.
Her voice had always drowned his, shut
down his manhood in a blistering fire,
and caught in his image, I cringed
for him, with him—withered, defeated,
the curdled wrath choking us both.

When he first left the house,
he fled through a hole of pain
out of which drained the thick phlegm
of their constant rage together.
The man was running for his life,
to see if he had one, if he was more than
the consequence of living with her.
When I'd see him—he'd moved
to another part of town—
the strain of doubt creased the skin
about his eyes and lips. Free
from the rounds of combat, still he
circled in fear on his long tether,
missing the half of himself
that was his own disease, this man,
this father in whose image
I measured my burgeoning self.

The lava still flows, it still flows,
And I look at my own children,
the oldest now fifteen, and I say:
I think we will make it through.
Our lives, troubled enough, have been
granted a different direction. Not
in our wisdom or our deserving
have my wife and I come this far,
for our unregarding words have struck
angriest sparks and our children
have suffered our rage. But our luck
has been holding; our private selves
have been fed within the boundaries
of our connection. And it will
make a difference . . . the difference.

(1981)

EASING DOWN TOWARD NICARAGUA

Christmas Week, 1984
Isla Mujeres, Mexico

To keep from burning I've leaned
my hot back against a white fishing boat.
There's a red stripe along its gunwales

El Nino Jesus hand-lettered in green
above the buried name of the co-op
that owns this boat belly-up on the beach.

Just off the shore a man untangles nets
and eats his lunch in the San Pedro Co-op's boat.
Its name is out to sea on the other side,

and the man's broad face that's brown and open
is Mayan, so it lets me picture again
the island's children at sun-up this morning:

children using only eyes at the *creche*
as they played untended with candles and sheep
and angels, and never touched. Here he and I,

unsure which of us might intrude, don't touch,
avoid each other's eyes as we squint now and then
across bright water to Cancun.

Surely he has spent some pocket-change pesos
once or twice on the little ferryboat
to see that place of awnings and tall hotels

that wasn't even there before the *gringoes*
came ten years ago. Clipped grass,
no dust or graves, no church,

no square where people sit in the shade
with cokes in that biggest town he ever saw.
As I squint into how he might see it, we are

suddenly speaking. Slowly. Like children.
His face moves like a wrinkled parable.
As our words play out line in jerks, he cleanly

slits behind the gill of a grouper
a quick bright string of blood.
He sells them, he says, only here on the island—

"to *La Pena*." That's the little cafe I like
facing into the cool dark square and the church
where the children wait for Christmas.

He washes down some bread by draining his cup
and as he refills it I want him to offer
his food and drink and feel terror that he might.

CHAPTER 30

What took you so long?

Sanity. Rational philosophy. Walking upright. The ice
on the driveway, vertigo, the broken strut—and the way
we had to shoot the animals. Inevitably, a glacier: find-
ing the crampons, losing the matches, frozen k-rations
and the Russian Jeep.

       Explosions at dawn and at evening.
Questions at headquarters, Mme. La Chaise and the tea
ritual. Circular stairs, distress in the mirrors, the zeroes,
the ampersands, tunnel vision. Later that day, the Ger-
man tourist who translated for us.

       Glass on the highway
—headlights and taillights—the loss of the verb, the
concept of distance, one country disappearing into an-
other. And always, on a radio in an empty square, the
old song: memory winding down like a clock. But
finally, and really, the loss of a landscape, the loss of a
motive, the night nurse, the graveyard shift. Rational.
Philosophy.

MOONWATCH

for Wallace Stevens

i.

The moon climbs out of the river.
A firefly stops his flight
beneath blood clouds
trailing for miles.

ii.

Once, my belly hung
heavy with an imperfect motion
as though the moon, angry
and rotund, avenged my kind
for the generations behind us.

iii.

Why are the Indian women
bowing before a temple light?
Do they know the moon
shrouds a mound, sacred
and well-hidden?

iv.

A man preparing to live
dies this way: climbing
into skies, swearing
the only light worth saving
is a delicate balance
he calls Moon.

v.

Children of Darkness, how long
have your eyes contained
the alterations of ancient moons?

vi.

The waters cover the shores tonight.
There is a Sea of Showers
in the moon's full light.

vii.

The moon crosses the ocean again.
Huntsmen lower their heads in prayer.

viii.

When a woman's blood
darkens with imbalance,
she knows there will be no
moon that night.

ix.

The moon hangs cold
where the Mothers lay their offerings
upon a sacrificial ground.

x.

All night, tribesmen chant their hymns;
the old moon pales in the new moon's arms.

xi.

Sister, I am here beside the garden path.
I watch your spirit ascending
among the dusk clouds.

xii.

By the sanctuary door, I place twelve
silver jars in an arc of moon color.
Overhead, watchmen turn their lantern
toward the earth.

THE WOMEN OF THE T2

wait at every bus stop
from Rockville to Bethesda
All along Great Falls Road
against the unfamiliar green
of Potomac's swollen hills,
they stand like Rivera figures
or forgotten sculptures
mixed from earth
coppers, yellows, browns
A mustard-colored scarf
falls behind one
like an old serape
Their eyes are dark
patient

They are out of their element
all of them
placed like Hopi dolls
in a long curve
Their bags
are not on their heads or backs
Their clothes hang on them
or stretch across vast breasts
but their bodies are perfect
as trees or boulders

Just as in the paintings
the sun is always going down
The burnt light
holds them in flat relief
against the hills
They are still
Their eyes watch for something
They have been waiting a long time

TRAINABLE

Somewhere he had learned the way
to explore womanly landscapes
ignoring hearsay of street-corner elders
who had blundered, blind-canyoned,
with great careless fingers.

Disowning the monotony of haste
as if it were out-of-date paisley luggage
he made the grand tour
headed for the less-observed attractions:
the ear's glen, the elbow's pocket
and that small hollow where hair and neck collide.
Here was a man with is own carnal Michelin guide.

A seasoned pilgrim no longer baffled
by topographical maps
he trusted his sense of direction,
moved down, up and around
alert to all trail signs she provided.

With the extravagance of the well-bred
he could wait for her
to settle into mouth-breathing,
cradle the question mark of her spine
till she shifted into stiffness.

BIOLOGY I

Coach chloroforms the hen.
A cotton wad soaked in fumes
sends the room spinning.
He opens the flipchart to
Half-Views of the Heart's
Four Chambers: Ventricle
Aorta. Left. Right.

We gather. See the muscle tick-
tock. In-out, a perfect pump,
open-close. "And now," he says,
"the sacrifice. From the Latin
sacrificium." And pouring ether
Thru stuffed beak. we see
the clock slow. Stop.

LAS

We are pink flowers on cactus stems,
spiky and succulent embers in spring;
we are grassy trails, desert headings;
we are a hot hot breath and dry calm.

We are the wasteland, the nightland
of coyotes and cowboys;
we are bright lights, laid-back leggy ladies;
we are waitress, gas attendant—
holes in the night;
we are the curves on a giant's chest.

We are high dusky days with insects
painted on our bumpers, we are spicy nights
with insects painted on our thighs;
we are vegas
            vegas
                vegas
                    vegas vegas!

WORDS HAVE SEX LIVES OF THEIR OWN

She undressed her words
so their bones would show
and joints would move
in unusual ways.
The words turned around,
they made love in her mouth.
What a coup for the language.
The chaste in the room
effervesced from their ears,
changed their minds
to erogenous zones.
Every sentence they spoke
knew a sensuous root,
every phrase
kept a sentence or two
on the side. Every word,
it was learned, had once squealed
with delight in the bed,
with delight in the bed of the mind.

from "DREAM COUPLINGS"

I	I
dream	am
	home
the	from
sloth	vacation,
is	sleeping
	in
a	our
dark	house
animal	on
	top
with	of
four	a
legs.	mountain.
It	
shoots	I
bullets	see
	a
out	golden
of	cross
its	descend
	on
nipples,	me,
because	but
I	I
	decide
didn't	not
love	to
	believe.
all	
of	
	Mom
the	is
people	upset
	cause
I	I
	didn't
was	make
supposed	my
to.	bed.

PROJECTILES

I

David prepares:
sling back,
band taut.

There is no drama:
the stone flies again,
the story is retold.

There is always victory in the stories of our creation.

II

Another sits,
patiently folding,
a classmate as his shield:

each angle straight,
each crease firm,
nose sharp and determined.

When she turns, the plane will be ready.

III

On the runway,
in the sling,
the passengers sit, strapped.

There is no red button,
no billowy white sheet
to unfold into safety:

there is only the flat space of the open sky.

AMPLIFICATION

They're never there when you need them—
I was so mad I couldn't see straight,
And I told that poetry workshop leader,
Don't you dare try to tell me
What amplification is.

On our little Carole's fifth birthday,
The first thing she said was
"I have a present for you, Mommie—
And Daddy, but you have to wait and see."

The first thing she did was
Swing her waking-up present,
A camera, by its carrying strap
And let go against the chimney.

After breakfast, she took her stereo
By the handle, whirled round and round,
And let fly against the picture window.

At her party she put presents in
A shopping bag and swung it around
With both hands letting it go
In the pool, the swimming pool.

Instead of napping, we discovered,
She had climbed upon the kitchen ladder
Fitted loose line around her neck
On the carousel clothes dryer
And swung around.

CABALLOS

*The Incas were less interested in killing the Spaniards than
in killing their horses. They feared the horses more.*
from a lecture on the Spanish conquests

At first when the conquerers came,
waving shields and pikes, plumes dancing,
we thought them brilliant birds,
but when they stripped to bathe
we saw they were not gods.
Under the feathers and scales,
their genitals hung down mournful and wrinkled,
and their bodies were hairy and pale.

They brought us The Word in a black book—
tiny letters writhing like centipedes
on every page, but it was the horses
that gave them power—*Caballos*, they called them—
backs like lintels, limbs striking fire
from stone as they ran. Browsing,
turning the grass into flesh. Even
their stools smelled sweet.

Although our gods were with us
at Cajamarca, their gods came
in the kingly flesh. The Spaniards galloped
on their borrowed bodies as a child
riding his father's shoulders
takes himself for a man. Thin men
on fat horses. Fat men on thin horses.
Riding our shoulders, they made themselves lords.

The first horse we killed,
we cut the head off.
Hung on the wall surrounded
by flowers, the head began to weep.
It told of the sadness in flesh,
but said nothing about the gods,
nothing to us who stood below
with offerings burning for words.

FUMBLE

In dreams
footballs
one-hop
back to you.
Stickum fingers
hang tight.
Willpower works.

But in games
where control
matters
the pigskin
changes shape
as though possessed,
and rolls
farther away
in slow motion
as the field
telescopes
and bodies
fall down.

SURGERY

I look down
long slender needle
dangles a bit left breast
walls x-ray room open
Roman scene shrieking rabble
soldiers bows taut
Sebastian amazed stares
first arrow juts from chest.

Operating room lights giant
discs great eyes shatter
explosion stained glass
shards emerald vermilion gold
drug wears off world
lump breast cutting
doctor another shot Aztec
priest incarnate chants
here take this to lab
holds my pouting heart to sun
I float over the table
gown incarnadine as
the blood-soaked rags.

1985

VERNAL EQUINOX, WASHINGTON, D.C. 1984

My father rode down that time's sky in a perfect
visioned dream, as if he had never been away. I
wanted to show him the nation's capital, but he
was here on other business; he wanted to find his
merchant marine papers, why, I don't know, but
perhaps to show passage through eternity and beyond;
a journey pulling toward yet another shore.
Look at the beautiful masonry, I say to him, look at
the Merchant Marine Building with its exquisite work
of brick and tile, and bronze doors, and frontispieces.
We went to a little section of a city by the sea
oh, I said to him, this is just like Italy, the marble
and the little streets and the glassworks and the women
who walk there, and the women he joked with, and the sailors,
and the bricklayers, and the carpenters, and the harvest
hands from Kansas long ago who passed in the street,
recognized by memory, composite in chirality, patient
in formality, they, the broad-faced and the rough-hewn
people, walking the narrow streets by outdoor cafes.
He knew where to go, not up the marbled entrance,
but down a side street near the building, where, stood
in the dried dust of the sea bottom, a small round
outdoor office with a woman behind the counter.
Draw me a picture of the last scene you remember
as a mariner, she said. He drew a picture of himself
sitting on a bed, his sailor's hat cocked to one
side, a coffee cup on the table. He asked her jokingly,
how do you want me, ma'm, hobbled and ironed? She
helped him look. How far back? He didn't know.
Down in the sea dust of bottom drawer they found
his papers waterstained brown. He pulled them out
and waved and yelled as if he had found passage,
like a youthful clown setting out on a new adventure.

ON THE ISLAND

1

The black coat is the Key to Fashion.
She wants it. The one with the collar
that won't quit, the mid-calf, wool, black coat:
the limit, the essence, half-price.
The black coat! She wants it.

She tries it. The perfect coat.
She is particular, precise.
She is the woman in the black coat.

See her seduce the Bay!
See her lie in iridescent foam!
The soft wool rides the waves.

She gives it back to the rack.

2

As she watches the boats
that go for clams and scallops,
the wind slaps her
the wind that wears kid gloves.
She has consumed many heads
of lettuce, she has picked
at many bones of fish.

She repeats a thousand motions.
She gathers her heart and body
at last, home, to the place
of her solitary choosing.

The seagulls wing before her window screen.
She wears her skin alone to bed.

MAINE SUMMER

After days of fog and a strong ocean
running, buoys clanging and foghorns groaning,
every visible thing fading into water-laden air,
the weather turned. That morning we picked
blueberries in sunlight striking
our backs, striking the sky luminous
as we looked up and saw, miles
out to sea, water breaking white
on the sharp cliffs on Pond Island, sails
brilliant as the wings of gulls
as they flashed from the waves.
That was the day our friend, far away, died.

We spent the summer idly, playing
with our daughter's small
hands, watching her gesture.
We painted the boat and repaired
the dock, strolled beaches for driftwood
and broken glass, the edges of marshes
for rosemary. We walked mudflats
to gather mussels and dig clams.
The water came in easily over the flats,
then inexorably, till the bay deepened
again, blue, inexplicable.

Our hands still smell of life plucked
from the sea. In sandcasts on the mantle
the mussel shells, iridescent, gleam.
Light catches the beachglass in a jar.
Here, too, the air burns bright. We remember

firs green as fire, our weeks-old daughter gazing
beyond them, a traveller meditating blue
horizons, the shores she came from, where
our friend has gone, childless, still young.

ON THE PATH TO THE OCEAN:
ON BEING ASKED TO CONSIDER
THE SOCIAL RESPONSIBILITY OF THE POET

Had I not been distracted by
the basso profundo frog in the swamp
and consequent digressions,

I would not have rescued
one rusted Budweiser can
and jagged slashes of styrofoam.

Had I not knelt by this murky pond
to catch some fairytale fish with the answers,
I'd have netted more than reflected clouds.

Had I not leaned over that slimy water
interflowing patterns
brown, green, mirrored blue,

I would not have seen
one hundred pre-metamorphic
non-metaphoric tadpoles

rippling the surface which,
physicists insist, does not move,
it's only energy making waves.

Had I not been diverted by
the territorially imperative
redwing blackbirds and dragonflies,

my freely associative imagination
captive to helicopters and ICBMs,
Vietnam, Iran, Salvador,

and by extension, my duty
to stave off more wars,
I would not have fallen in.

Which shows that however noble
or pure our intent—
to pursue what is pure, like oceans—

it's danger, stagnation and trash,
and sloth in the Maytime sun
that draw us in, or down.

Also the flash
of ephemeral ripple and wing,
and the bullfrog's pride.

St. Mary's–1983

GREAT MOTHER

I see a shadow
That looks like a tree
Moving from limb and root
Laboring / lumbering forward
Feet apart
Arms at reach
There are fish
Hanging from each palm
Their erratic life dances
Look like leaves in a breeze
I see children scaling Her trunk
Emerging in birth
From Her bleeding side
Slick-skinned like fish
I hear Her children chanting like wind
Mouths opening for gasps of breath
Their erratic life dances
Look like leaves
Hanging from bleeding palms
Hanging from lumbering limbs
Children become fish
Fish become children
like blood touched leaves
Sustained

A REPORT TO THE LIBRARY BOARD

I never was one to carry tales,
but something's got to be done
to protect the little children of this county.
The person, I'll not call her a lady,
who's driving the bookmobile like it's a jet,
Doreen Sutphun, is my complaint.
My teensie grandson, Harry Joe, is earning a
gold star for every book he reads during vacation.
Today I let him go by hisself to get his books.
He come back home crying
that a man was fighting Doreen on the bookmobile.
I run up there without even putting on my face,
and you can believe me, it won't no fight going on.
It was sin-ful for-ni-ca-tion in the aisle
with all them wonderful books looking on.
I was brought up to respect the printed word.
I regard what I saw as sacrilegious.
That hussy was carrying on with Atlas Demphy,
young man so involved with weight lifting.
His muscles ain't the only thing swelled up.
He's got a head to match. So stuck-up.
Now I ask you, are taxpayers supposed to pay
for employees to do this kinda thing on our time?
Doreen better work at the desk in the main library.
She needs to be on display, circulating,
not on reserve in some back room.

UP EARLY READING YANG WAN-LI

This old zen joker had the right idea.
One day he's drunk on rice wine
and falling down among the flowers.
The next day he won't take a drink and says–
"Who knows what it means to really get high."

He takes long naps in his river boat
and writes poems when the mood strikes him.
When he's depressed
the smell of young orchids revives him.

In youth he grew thin by the reading lamp,
now he shouts "Don't read books"
and turns his face to the rain.

It's a long way from Sung China
to the shores of Turtle Island,
but this old zen bum
is a brother under the skin.

THE HOUSE VIRGINIA WOOLF KNEW

Silver waters lap at the pilings,
derelict now as lost ports,
nothing there but eel grass and seaweed
alien to an inland woman.
They whisper seductively
as they weave back and forth in the wind.

She sees that mussels stick down in the dank mud
at the edge of the water
like ebony daggers
She hears an osprey scream from its nest
on an umber post
just out of her reach
over there beyond the jagged oyster flats
at the rim of the sky.
The grass speaks to her, saying,
again and again,
Welcome, walk in, walk in,
and out to the place where the terns cry.

You will find a place of your own there,
a room in the deep,
down where the old sirens lived
and tired women who write poems sleep—
the house Virginia Woolf knew.

A STREET CAR CONDUCTOR, NEW ORLEANS, 1915

This from my father as witness:
An old man, he said, walrus-mustached,
Would loudly call each stop, as duty demanded,
And the car clanking up St. Charles, approaching
The streets so wonderfully named for the Greek muses,
"CAL-LI-OPE!" he would shout,
Pronouncing it so to the local understanding,
But would add, in a low aside,
"Really Cal-lie-'o-pee."
And so to "MEL-POE-MEEN!" and his soft correction:
"Should be Mel-pom-'e-nee."
Easy to see him an old ham actor,
This public instruction put on just to amuse.
I see him rather a proud fifth century Roman
Surrounded by Goths, the defender of classical culture,
The preserver of language against the barbarians.
hear him down through time:
"TERP-SI-KORE!" And then the low admonition:
"Call it Terp-sik-'o-ree."

THE OFFERING

She said the floral
arrangement was a memento
so I would have something
to remember her by
when she is gone.

> *Mama, please don't spank me*
> *again. I won't wet my bed*
> *again. I promise.*

She knew she didn't have
long to live and these
yellow flowers would be a
remembrance.

> *Mama, don't lock me in*
> *the closet again. Oh*
> *please let me out. I will*
> *be good. I promise.*

The yellow plastic flowers
look so beautiful in the
yellow plastic vase and
they will last a long time—
longer than the real ones.

> *Mama, don't burn my fingers*
> *with those matches.*
> *I won't ever take anything*
> *without asking, again.*
> *I promise.*

Whenever you look at them
you can think of me, she said.

> *Mama, he only kissed me.*
> *I won't let him do anything*
> *more than that.*
> *I promise. . . .*

Plastic yellow flowers
in a plastic yellow vase
somehow look just right
on your grave, mama.

> *I won't ever forget.*
> *I promise.*

THE CHICKEN REFUSES TO CROSS THE ROAD

for Peter Klappert

And then the telegrams sent
one after another like cloud breaths
until the answer becomes self-evident:
the chicken refuses to cross the road
spills tremolos of nonsense.
Who keeps a journal of such things
who the sculpture

                  the stand
with watches!

The notion of living is taken up
              but the way to it
has grown more difficult.

It may be thoughts have wandered
too long in a tedium, not paying us
there as a forest preserve instead.
Nevertheless, day has come up gracious
and the small green bud in the room

        can be counted on to open.

AUGUST 4, 1983

I cannot tell
why memory feeds upon secret wells
where desires are not dead but sleep
and leap at the strangest summons.

Blue swells flowing on the frail
hands of a Russian emigré
call to mind your long slender hand
offering Fraülein Elizabeth and me
Heller candies in the Prater;

or leaves slow pattering
behind my shoulders
are ever your soft laughter
at a Mantua circus, reassuring me
frightened by a clown.

A long farewell lingers
between you and me, Father,
an unfinished gesture, lifting a curtain
over a desolate inner landscape

where your image seems held back,
color thinned, outlines distorted,
fragments fleeting in an insubstantial
medium. I have grown accustomed
to your fading away, and the seeming peace
of not being certain of what we were
or if we were at all, outside of one another.

Today you would be eighty-six.
There is in my well a falling
of evergreens, lichens, mosses—
in my landscape a surfing of shadows.

GREEN SPRINGS THE TREE

My young son lurches halfway down the stair
or shrieks and totters midway through a climb
from the wobbling bookcase to the rocking chair.
I freeze and hold my breath. Most of the time
I am too far away to break the fall
that seldom comes. Instead, I stoop and bend
with him, as if threads of remote control
could reel out and connect him to my hand
that strains against his fall, against my leap
to rescue him. My twisting body prays
for skill in this, the high wire he will keep
both of us on as we rehearse the ways
to braid these strands of our inheritance
and teach poor body english how to dance.

SHREDDING THE EVIDENCE: AUGUST 1980

To stand on the pier in Annapolis is
to doubt the bad news. Summer is here again

and French turistas
stroll up the avenue. Everyone's

stripped to the waist and taken to boats,
gazing into blue skies, entering

this monumental era of good feelings.
Or sunk in the mindless lyrics of

loving and leaving. Here there is
something for everyone. Everything's

up for grabs. *Ah, this is the life.*
Just for once to lose sight of shore

as those tiny figures, landlocked and sweltering,
drift out of sight, to speak

in the smooth tongue of an idle vacationing soul
getting an eyeful. As a man in his middle years,

forgetful and human, murmurs *ready about*, then
blunders again into a little breeze, the lull

of the forward motion, the lull of the backward glance.

RETURN VOYAGE
TO MARY-LAND:
A NEW RIME
OF THE ANCIENT
POET LAUREATE

in the voice of Ebenezer Cooke, gent.

I knew you would say it was not very grand,
My satiric first poem about Mary-land.
But why blame the victim for becoming sore
And using his verse to settle the score—
When you stole my money and threw me out of court
And laughed when I left your ancient port
With my clenched fist curse that your lands go waste
Where no man's faithful or any woman chaste.

That was, after all, three centuries ago
And many other furrows we've all had to hoe.
Without rancor I return with my ink and my pen
To describe the improvements you've made since then.
But—may heaven forgive me—the effect of my curse
Has been to drive you from bad to worse!

Returned I here on a Concorde plane
Through clouds and clouds of acid rain.
Beneath me the Bay, once perfectly blue,
Is thick now with algae and industrial goo.
When inland I go, what do I see
But cement cities and nowhere a tree.

When first I came here for career in barter
You stole my shoes and then my garters.
In place of tobacco you sold me dry grasses

And left me in tears as thick as molasses.
Today when I ask what you have for sale,
You say politicians fresh out of jail.
When I say I am wary of buying more grass,
You say you've some SPEED that supercedes gas.
When I explain I'm a poet and well-known bard,
You say you have sufficient Hallmark cards.
Well, I don't blame you for looking down at the arts,
At the end of your nose you've nothing but warts.
Thy native poets, like Edgar Poe,
Need cocaine and pot to make their words glow.
True, some of thy poets write with less frills,
Like thy laureate who read us his laundry bills.

> So farewell again, again it's adieu,
> I won't return for an eon or two—
> Since I see you need a little more time
> To overcome the curse of my ancient rime.

SIMPLE

He pruned images from trees
and discarded nature poems,
chased animals from under rocks,
and wrote essays about reason.
He banished ghosts from the family attic,
and when he thought he was ready,
he sorted childhood toys and sent them away;
they kept coming back uninvited.

He married a career but was afraid
of heights and longed to go home
to mother. He viewed himself
at the center of a city built
just for him, but there were days
when the walls came tumbling down
and he saw the work of a lifetime
in ruins laid out before him.

He worried about the condition
of the world and searched for answers.
The sun and moon and stars
were accounted for, but nobody
could explain war,
how ideas become ossified,
why brother hates brother,
or how love suddenly ends.

He made a list of paradoxes,
wrote them into equations,
but the factors were too variable
and nothing came out right.
Then fear crept out of quarantine

at night and painted dark abstractions
fracturing the rim of the real world
as he thought he understood it.

Unable to write about what he knew
he would never be able to know,
he sat under the twisted trees
with amputated limbs and wrote
poems about childhood and nursery rhymes
that kept coming back,
that wouldn't leave him alone,
that made everything seem simple.

SMALLMOUTHS

All I see are tails
waving through the water,
and circles that startled frogs
began in their descents.
The circles, according to poets,
widen into forever.
I could never think of that.
I think rather of you—
the way your eyes seem circles
that change into skies—
the way chestnut hair
loosens on your shoulders.
I think of this by a lake
darkened with low clouds.
Lulled on a rock,
I swallow the horizon
with the motion fish breathe—
until their drifting tails
seem to wave goodbye
as the slender smallmouth bass
shoal in deeper water.

LONGING

In the hot days of summer
I long for echoes of my shadow

In the fields of the meadow
I search for lilies and daisies
And longing to hear on my pillow

The jangles of horses and
Nightsongs of insects and birds

In the cold days of winter
I long and I hope
For the love of my dream

To sprinkle my heart and tiresome flesh
With his touch and caresses

At nightfall
When silence and darkness
Perceives all my sorrow

I long for the breast of my mother
To cryout my hurt and my plea

I search for the hands of my father
To lift me far as can be

And yet, through my window
I still can hear. . . .

The whispering Love of shadowy trees
Calling me gently

"You are a sparrow
But we care for *ti*."

JOE LEE

Joe Lee, you are a leader, indeed.
You were motivated to run and win, motivated to succeed.
You motivated others to take a positive lead.

We set out to prove that you, a Black man, could be
The first Black sheriff in our county.
We proved it Joe, it was wonderful fate.
You were not just the first in the county.
But the whole darn state.

You campaigned hard and pulled out voters by the score.
You shook hands as you went door to door.
But the most wonderful thing, the most beautiful sight to see,
Was all that togetherness in the Black Community.

You were the stimulus for this unity, the catalyst, the fire
And for this we all thank you for creating a desire.
A desire to lead, a desire to succeed, succeed!

Every community needs a "Joe Lee," a motivating force.
A strong courageous someone, from which comes our energy source.
That source is hope for our people,
That has always been plain to see.
And you, Joe Lee, join forces with "Great Black Men"
Who are now part of history.

This poem was written not as a celebration of former Sheriff Joe Lee Somerville's victory, but as a tribute to him after his loss in the acrimonious election of 1982.

CIRCLING

The balance shifts.
The sea striped ball
begins to roll away from summer.

Like an animal
feeling his coat thicken,
I am restless
for change.

The grass,
burned out,
is a tough brindled pelt.
The leaves are chewed,
patched with brown darns.

Empty as envelopes,
lists scratched on their backs,
days drag,

and die.
The tattered wings
of butterflies
are the color of old pennies.

The Land Mary-land

WORDS and MUSIC © 1987 by Tom Wisner

DEDICATED TO GOVERNOR HARRY HUGHES
WHOSE LEGISLATIVE PROGRAM FOR THE BAY
IS A POETRY OF ITS OWN, UNEQUALED IN
OUR REGIONAL HISTORY.

CHORUS: MODERATELY

OH THE LAND, MAR-Y-LAND WILL SURE-LY RE-VEAL

A PLACE TO BE-LIEVE IN THE TRUTH THAT WE FEEL.

ON THE WINGS OF THE MORN-ING IN THE CUP OF HIS HAND,

WE WILL CAR-RY OUR LONG-ING TO THE FAIR MAR-Y-LAND.

VERSE:

1. A-MID ROPE TAR AND CAN-VAS AND TORN FROM OUR PAST,
2. SHE IS RIGGED OUT AND HAND-SOME A MAID OF THE SEA,
3. LONG BE-FORE I WAS MADE IN THE DEPTHS OF THE EARTH,

1. IN A DUN-GEON OF TIM-BER WE PRAY WE MAY LAST
2. BOUND ON A JOUR-NEY FOR HU-MAN-I-TY.
3. YOU KNEW OF MY LONG-ING AND YOU FASH-IONED MY BIRTH,

1. THROUGH SICK-NESS AND TUR-MOIL IN SEARCH OF OUR HOME,
2. SHE'LL SAIL THROUGH THE MORN-ING TO THE GREAT O-CEAN WIDE,
3. WITH A PAS-SION TO JOUR-NEY OUT O-VER THE SEA

1. WE WILL TRUST OUR CON-VIC-TION TO THE ROL-LING WHITE FOAM.
2. BEAR-ING THE LONG-ING THAT IS CAR-RIED IN-SIDE.
3. IN SEARCH OF THE VIS-ION OF THE RIGHT TO LIVE FREE.

Karren LaLonde Alenier founded and has been director of the Miller Cabin Poetry Series and Poet's Jam. Two collections of her poetry, *The Dancer's Muse*, and *Wandering on the Outside*, have been published as well as the anthology, *Whose Woods These Are*, which she edited.

Mary Azrael has taught as a Poet-in-the Schools. She is also a free lance journalist. Her poems have appeared in such publications as *Prairie Schooner, Harper's,* and *Poet Lore*. Her first book, *Victorians*, came out in 1982.

William Barnes grew up on the plains of West Texas, spent a while on the sea and now lives among the oaks, hickories and poplars of Southern Maryland.

James H. Beall is a widely respected astrophysicist whose biography first appeared in *Who's Who in the World* in 1985. He is a member of the faculty at St. John's College in Annapolis. His poems have been published widely, and his book, *Hickey, The Day*, was published by Word Works, Inc.

David Beaudouin is a native of Baltimore, where he lives and writes and loves. He is the founder and editor of Tropos Press which publishes *The Pearl*, Baltimore's oldest independent journal of the literary and visual arts.

Anne Becker lives in Takoma Park, Maryland with her husband and young son. She is currently working on a manuscript of poems in the voices of Charles and Emma Darwin. A selection of these recently appeared in *Gargoyle*. Anne also works with The Watershed Foundation's Poets' Audio Center.

Marguerite Beck-Rex of Silver Spring, Maryland has been a journalist and a member of the Big Mama Poetry Troupe. She has won two national awards for news writing and the Susan B. Anthony Award for work by local women. Her poems have appeared in numerous journals and anthologies.

Marc Lawrence Britt, a native of Virginia, holds an M.A. in British literature, teaches occasionally at St. Mary's College of Maryland and has worked as an editor for Tracor, Inc. He is currently studying for the Episcopal priesthood. His home is in Dameron, Maryland.

Tammy Chapman, a native of St. Mary's County, MD, has engaged in the study of Jungian-Senoi dreamwork therapy and earned an MSW at Florida State University. She works with the visually impaired, writes and lives with her daughter, Rhee, in Florida from where she reports she is reaping what she's sown.

Maxine Clair teaches creative writing at the American University and The Ellington High School for the Arts in D.C. Her work has appeared in various publications including *Gargoyle, The Washington Review of the Arts,* and *Folio.*

J. Wesley Clark is an Annapolis-born poet, prose writer, and journalist. He edited *The Thursday Book: Selected Poetry from the Dove Readings.* His poems have appeared widely, and his collection, *Daughter of the South Country*, was published by Free State Press in 1979.

Shirley Graves Cochrane, a native of Chapel Hill, lives in D.C. where she teaches writing courses at Georgetown. Her first book, *Burnsite*, was published by Washington Writers' Publishing House. *Family and Other Strangers*, her second collection of poems, was just published by Word Works, Inc.

Rhea L. Cohen is a politically active environmentalist who has studied journalism, literature and archaeology. She has published in such magazines and anthologies as *Bellingham Review, The Swallow's Tale, The Ear's Chamber,* and *Black Box,* and her chapbook, *Message from Mid-River*, appeared in 1980.

George Herman Coppage, who studied at Washington College, Howard University and Temple University, is a former clergyman, teacher, social worker and cab dispatcher. He is now retired and writing in Lexington Park, Maryland.

Sarah Cotterill studied at the Iowa Writers' Workshop and has been a Yaddo Fellow. Her work has appeared in *A.P.R., Poetry Northwest* and *Ploughshares*, etc., and in Sleeping Bird Press's chapbook, *The Hive Burning*. She is a MD Arts Council grant recipient and teaches at the Writer's Center in Bethesda.

Frank Evans was born into a Southern Molasses Dialect. He migrated to New England where he developed a slight twang with a distinct medical-scientific aroma to it. Later, on the analytic couch, he discovered iambic pentameter as his mother tongue. Thirty years in Maryland have lent a touch of Chesapeake, and put a "T" in Balt-Tee-Mure.

Robert Farr sees poetry as primarily an oral art form, brought to life through performance. He sees himself as writing in the Beat tradition, inspired by Kerouac, O'Hara and others. Farr lives in Washington, D.C.

Roland Flint has published a chapbook and three volumes of his poetry, the most recent being *Resuming Green: Selected Poems, 1965-1982* (New York: The Dial Press, 1983). He teaches literature and writing at Georgetown University.

Mary A. Gaumond is an active member of the Maryland State Poetry and Literary Society and has served as president of both it and the district branch of the National League of American Pen Women. She lives in Bowie, Maryland with her husband Paul.They have three married children.

Patricia Garfinkel works on Capitol Hill as a speech writer. Her poems have been published in such magazines and anthologies as *The Hollins Critic, Cedar Rock, Washingtonian, Window,* and *American Classic.* Her chapbook, *Ram's Horn*, was published in 1980. She lives in Reston, Virginia.

Michael S. Glaser, director of the Ebenezer Cooke Poetry Festival, teaches literature and creative writing at St. Mary's College of Maryland. He recently returned from sabbatical study in Oxford, England where he was invited to give a reading by the Oxford University Poetry Society.

Barbara Goldberg has an MFA from American University where she currently teaches. A recipient of many awards, including an N.E.A. grant and Pen Syndicated Fiction award, she has published widely. Her new book, *Berta Broadfoot and Pepin the Short: a Merovingian Romance*, was published by Word Works, Inc. and The Porcupine's Quill.

Judith Hall has received grants from the Ingram Merrill Foundation and the Maryland State Arts Council. She has been a Fellow at Yaddo and McDowell and has taught at SMCM, Loyola and for PITS. Her poems have appeared in *The Antioch Review, Nimrod,* and *Shenandoah*, among others.

William Heath has published poems, essays, stories and reviews in a wide variety of little magazines, literary quarterlies and anthologies. He teaches American literature and creative writing at Mount St. Mary's College in Emmitsburg, MD.

Paul Hopper was born in Washington, D.C. For eight years he taught German and related subjects at Penn State University. Since 1981 he has been a translator for the federal government.

Gray Jacobik lives in Groton, Massachusetts where she writes, teaches and is a Ph.D. candidate at Brandeis University. Widely published, she has recent work in *The Hollins Critic* and the *Worcester Review*. Her third book, *Sand-Painting*, was published by Washington Writers' Publishing House.

Philip K. Jason has been published in many literary magazines and journals. His two collections of poetry, *Thawing Out*, and *Near the Fire* are both published by Dryad Press. Jason teaches at the United States Naval Academy and is co-editor of *Poet Lore*.

Rod Jellema began writing poetry at age 40. He has since published three books of poetry: *Something Tugging the Line, The Lost Faces*, and *The Eighth Day*. He has also published a volume of poetry translated from Frisian, *Country Fair: Poems from Friesland since 1945*.

Peter Klappert directs the graduate writing program at George Mason University. His first book, *Lugging Vegetables to Nantucket*, was published as the 1971 Yale Series of Younger Poets award. His most recent book, *The Idiot Princess of the Last Dynasty*, was published by Knopf.

Carolyn Kreiter-Kurylo is a painter, sculptor and poet. She has won several awards for her poetry and has published poetry and articles on writing in such magazines as *Antioch Review, Wind, English Journal, Artemis*, and *Roanoke Review*.

Mary Ann Larkin is a poet, teacher, free-lance writer and fund raiser. A founding member of the Big Mama Poetry Troupe, she has published in such collections as *The Other Side of the Hill, The Poet Upstairs, The Ear's Chamber*, and *Harbor Lights*. Her book, *The Coil of Skin*, was published in 1982 by WWPH.

Lenny Lianne, a native Washingtonian who currently lives in Alexandria, has read widely in the D.C. area. Her poems have appeared in *Bogg, Bay Window, Cat's Eye, Friendly Woman, Up Against the Wall, Mother* and elsewhere. She conducts writing workshops in "reclaiming your own story."

Chris Llewellyn has been published in various anthologies and journals. In 1985 she was Poet-In-Residence at the Festival of Poets and Poetry at St. Mary's College, and in 1986 won the Walt Whitman Award of the AAP for her narrative poem, *Fragments From the Fire*, recently published by Viking Penguin.

Jessica Frances Locklear was spirited away from the Superstition Mountains in Arizona on a moonless night many years ago. Since that time her mortal form has appeared in Baltimore in a book of poems, *Illusioning*. Her soul remains stranded on the highways of America.

Elaine Magarrell has published poetry in *The Literary Review, Poet Lore, Yankee, Folio* and other journals. Her book, *On Hogback Mountain*, won the publication prize from Washington Writers' Publishing House in 1984.

Chris Mason and Ellen Carter have been writing poems collaboratively since 1974. A tape of their work, *Ignorant Translations* is available from Widemouth Tapes in Baltimore, and a book of two-voice poems, *Dream Coupling* is forthcoming from Air Heart Press in Silver Spring, Maryland.

Richard E. Miller teaches at the College of Basic Studies, Boston University where he is working on a collection of poems entitled *This Is Interesting*.

Warren C. Miller has published extensively in literary magazines and anthologies. His collection of short stories, *A Small Town is Best for Waiting and Other Stories* was published by Climate Books. At 61, he is "searching for the closing epigramatic couplet, anticipating a rejection slip."

Jean Nordhaus has published her work in numerous literary magazines. A chapbook of her poems, *A Language of Hands*, was published by SCOP in 1982, and her most recent book, *A Bracelet of Lies* was published by Washington Writers' Publishing House. She lives in Washington, D.C.

Richard Peabody is a Washington, D.C. native who has been the editor/publisher of *Gargoyle Magazine* since its inception in 1976. His book of poems is entitled *I'm In Love With The Morton Salt Girl/Echt & Ersatz*. He teaches fiction writing at St. John's College in Annapolis, Maryland.

Kathy Pearce-Lewis lives in Wheaton, MD and is a member of the Writer's Center in Bethesda. Her poems and reviews have appeared in *Rye Bread, Second Rising, Bogg, Poetry at the Angel, Visions, The Dog River Review*, etc. She has given frequent poetry readings in the Washington, D.C. area.

Charles Plymell is a Kansas-born, San-Francisco-bred poet, fiction writer and teacher with an MFA from Johns Hopkins University. Widely published, his books include *Last of The Moccasins* and *Trashing of America.* Plymell is publisher of Cherry Valley Editions.

Jacklyn Potter, a child TV star, received her MFA (with honors) from American University. Her poetry has won grants and prizes and has been published in various journals such as *Sou'wester, Washington Review of the Arts,* and *Black Box Magazine.* Her first book, *The Groaning Bed*, is expected soon.

Nancy Prothro is a Poet-in-the-Schools in Maryland and an assistant professor at the United States Naval Academy. She served as an editor and has published her poems in various journals and magazines.

Elisavietta Artamonoff Ritchie, writer, poet, translator, teacher and editor, has published five books of poetry, won numerous awards, grants and publication prizes, and has given readings, workshops and lectures worldwide. Her most recent book is *T is for Tomato: An Alphabet of Eating Poems.*

Alma Roberts lives in Baltimore and is the founder and president of New Breezes Cultural Arts Forum. She has been published in area anthologies and has read her work around the state of Maryland, the District of Columbia, and recently at the Nyumuburu Cultural Center as part of their Distinguished Poet Series.

Marie Kennedy Robins, burned out as a teacher, fled from suburbia to North Carolina, but still spends the warm months enjoying the sunsets over the Potomac in Southern Maryland. She began to write four years ago.

Charles Rossiter is past editor of *Third Coast Archives*. His latest book is *Thirds*, published by Distant Thunder Press. He occasionally teaches courses about the beat generation and beat writing, and enjoys working on his tan when he gets a chance.

Irene Rouse, after a lifetime of living in Northern Virginia where she directed the Prince Street Poetry Reading Series, now lives on a saltwater farm on the Eastern Shore of Maryland where she writes and sells antiquarian books.

Robert Sargent, a warmly valued fixture in Washington poetry affairs, has been published in many periodicals and has three books of poetry: *Now is Always the Miraculous Time, A Woman from Memphis,* and *Aspects of a Southern Story.* He is a MacDowell Colonist and a Virginia Center for Creative Arts Fellow.

Jayne Landis Silva is a former assistant to the Secretary, U.S. International Trade Commission. She has received several awards for her poetry and short stories and has been published in numerous magazines and anthologies. She currently is working toward a degree in English Literature at the U. of Maryland.

Susan Sonde has received MSAC and NEA grants, been a fellow at the Virginia Center for the Creative Arts, and won the Poetry Society of America's Gordon Barber Memorial Award. Her publication credits include *New Letters, Epoch,* and *Poet Lore.* Her chapbook, *Inland is Parenthetical*, is published by Dryad Press.

Elizabeth Sullam was born in Italy. She attended the University of Bologna and has also studied in London and at the American University. She is retired and lives and writes in Washington, D.C. Her work has been published in numerous anthologies and literary magazines.

Henry Taylor, of Lincoln, Virginia, is the director of the Graduate Writing Program at American University. His books of poetry include *The Horse Show at Midnight, Breakings, An Afternoon of Pocket Billiards*, and his 1986 Pulitzer Prize-winning collection, *The Flying Change.*

Margot Treitel lives in Columbia, Maryland. She has given several poetry readings at several locations in the area, including the Folger Library and Loyola College, and has most recently published in SCOP's *American Classic* anthology, *College English, The Literary Review* and *Hollins Critic.*

Ralph Treitel studied poetry with John Crowe Ransom at Kenyon College. He produces the *Little Patuxent Review* in Columbia and Howard County, Maryland, and has also had dramatic and video works presented on WMAR-TV, Baltimore's Artscape Festival, Baltimore's Playwrights Festival and Howard Cable T.V.

Stacy Tuthill is the founder of SCOP Publications, Inc. and now serves as its president. She has authored two books, *Postcards from Zambia,* and *Notes from a Learning Factory.* Her poetry and short stories have been published in numerous literary magazines and anthologies.

H.L. Lloyd Van Brunt now lives in Manhattan. His last two books, *FOR LUCK: Poems 1962–1977* and *And the Man Who Was Traveling Never Got Home,* were published by Carnegie-Mellon University Press. Most recently he has appeared in *Poetry Now, New Letters, Blueline, Confrontation* and *Pulpsmith.*

Rida von Luelsdorff was born in Cianking Province, China, and spent nine years of her childhood in a prison camp during the Stalin regime. At 17 she made her way to the U.S.A. She has earned B.S. and M.S. degrees from Georgetown U., published poems and articles and is interested in St. Brendan the Navigator.

Janice Walthour is the principal of Carver Elementary School in St. Mary's County, MD, where she has been a lifetime resident. Her poems have appeared often in local publications and she is well known in the tri-county area for her readings/renderings of black poetry.

Tom Wisner, a conservation educator, entertainer, writer and artist, has recorded two albums (Folkways): *Chesapeake Born*, and *(We've Got to) Come Full Circle*. Featured in the National Geographic's special, "Chesapeake Borne," he is currently finishing a textbook, *Life In and Around Chesapeake Bay.*

Mary Doughery Wood, a resident of Queen Anne's County, Maryland for the past 42 years, has been active in numerous civic organizations. Her plays, poems and short stories have been widely published and have won a number of grants, awards and prizes. From 1976–1981 she was active in the Maryland PITS program.

Acknowledgement is made to the following publications which first published some of the poems in this book:

Ohio Renaissance Review for Tammy Mae Chapman's "The Clam Bar;" *Termino* for J. Wesley Clark's "Souls in Pain;" *American Poetry Review* for Sarah Cotterill's "Among Other Places They Leave Their Bodies;" *Friends of the Library, North Carolina Wesleyan College* for Roland Flint's "Still" (which also was co-winner of the Maryland Heritage Poetry Competition); *Passage* for Mary A. Gaumond's "The Enchanted Forest;" *Chester H. Jones Foundation* for Michael S. Glaser's "Arm;" *The American Scholar* for Barbara Goldberg's "A Question of Aesthetics;" *Circular Stairs, Distress in the Mirrors* (The Griffin Press), copyright 1975 by Peter Klappert, reprinted by permission of the author, for Peter Klappert's "What Took You So Long?;" *Alexandria Penwomen* who awarded first place to Carolyn Kreiter-Kurylo for her poem, "Moonwatch;" *Finding The Name* (Wineberry Press) and *On Hogback Mountain* (Washington Writers' Publishing House) for Elaine Magarrell's "Words Have Sex Lives of Their Own;" *West Branch* for Jean Nordhaus's "Caballos;" *Washington Book Review* for Richard Peabody's "Fumble;" *The Christian Science Monitor* for Elisavietta Ritchie's "On the Path to the Ocean;" *The Flying Change* (L.A. State U. Press) for Henry Taylor's "Green Springs the Tree," copyright 1985 by Henry Taylor, reprinted by permission of the author; *Cincinnati Poetry Review* for Margot Treitel's "Shredding the Evidence: August, 1980;" *The Baltimore Sun* for Ralph Treitel's "Return Voyage to Mary-land;" *Long Pond Review* and *And The Man Who Was Traveling Never Got Home* (Carnegie-Mellon University Press) for H.L. Van Brunt's "Smallmouths;" *The Enterprise* for Janice Walthour's "Joe Lee."

THE COOKE BOOK: A Seasoning of Poets is set in 10 pt. ITC Garamond by Barbara Shaw. Special thanks to Charles Rossiter, Stephanie Demma and Stacy Tuthill for organizing and proofreading.